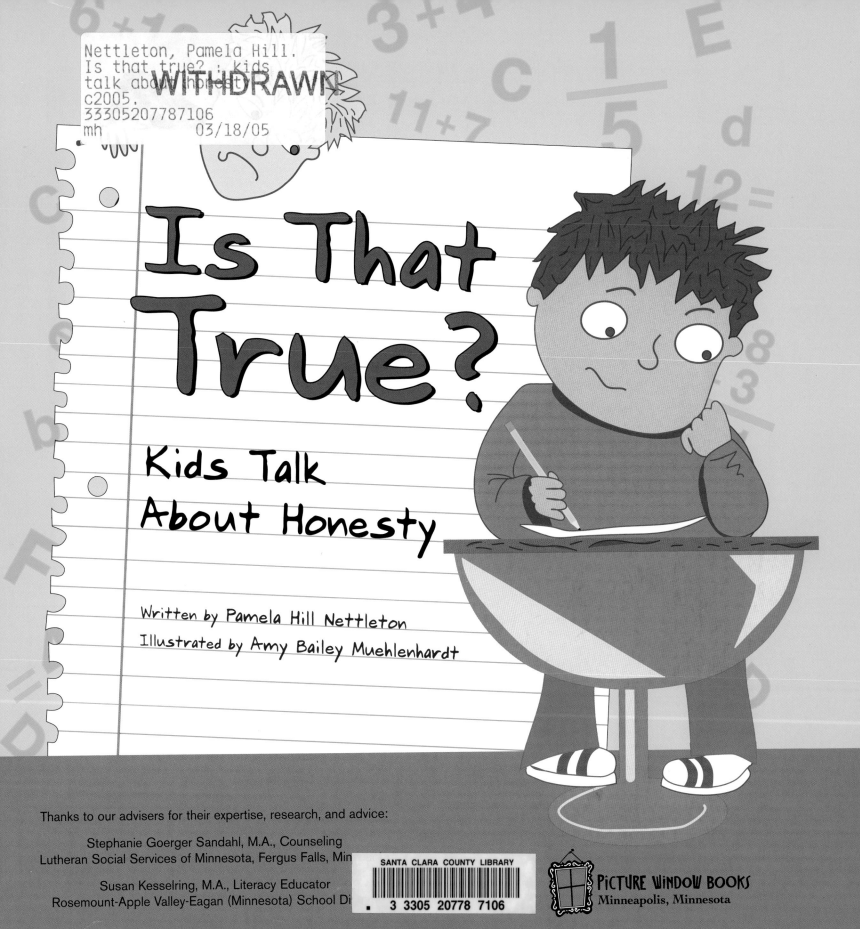

Is That True?

Kids Talk About Honesty

Written by Pamela Hill Nettleton

Illustrated by Amy Bailey Muehlenhardt

Thanks to our advisers for their expertise, research, and advice:

Stephanie Goerger Sandahl, M.A., Counseling
Lutheran Social Services of Minnesota, Fergus Falls, Min...

Susan Kesselring, M.A., Literacy Educator
Rosemount-Apple Valley-Eagan (Minnesota) School Di...

PICTURE WINDOW BOOKS
Minneapolis, Minnesota

Managing Editors: Bob Temple, Catherine Neitge
Creative Director: Terri Foley
Editors: Brenda Haugen, Christianne Jones
Editorial Adviser: Andrea Cascardi
Designer: Nathan Gassman
Page production: Picture Window Books
The illustrations in this book were rendered digitally.

Picture Window Books
5115 Excelsior Boulevard
Suite 232
Minneapolis, MN 55416
877-845-8392
www.picturewindowbooks.com

Printed in the United States of America.

Library of Congress Cataloging-in-Publication Data
Nettleton, Pamela Hill.
Is that true? : kids talk about honesty / written by Pamela Hill Nettleton ;
    illustrated by Amy Bailey Muehlenhardt.
p. cm. – (Kids talk)
Includes bibliographical references and index.
ISBN 1-4048-0619-9 (reinforced library binding : alk. paper)
1. Honesty–Miscellanea–Juvenile literature. I. Muehlenhardt, Amy Bailey, 1974-
    II. Title. III. Series.

BJ1533.H7N48 2004
179'.9–dc22
                                                        2003028241

To my children, Gretchen,
Christopher, and Ian,
who give the best advice

Dear Sam,

I know what it feels l...
one left out. Here's ...

This one time I knew ...
and he was really fu...
jokes. We all were ab... Keep
these things in min... st great!

Thanks for writi...

Frank B. W...

4

Hi! I'm Frank B. Wize, a 13-year-old guy who loves to read about your problems and give advice. I guess I figure what I've learned from making mistakes all these years should help someone, right?

I have a great English teacher here at C. U. Fidget Middle School who told my class something pretty cool. She said, "Adults make mistakes, too. Since we are older than you, we've had time to make a lot more of them. That's how we learn."

My English teacher was being honest. Being honest doesn't always win you friends or make people feel comfortable. Even if it's hard to do, being honest is still better than lying.

Let's talk about honesty for a while. I have a stack of letters here from kids like you. Read ahead, and see if you think I've learned anything from my mistakes.

Sincerely,

Frank B. Wize

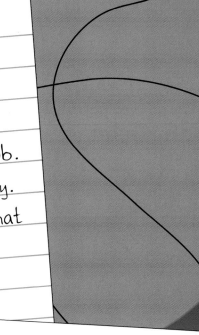

Dear Frank,

My mom asked if I broke a glass. I dropped the glass, but I told her one of my friends did it. When she asked which friend, I made up a friend named Bob. Now my mom asks me questions about Bob every day. I keep answering her, but now I can't remember what I've told her. What should I do?

Steven

Dear Steven,

Buddy, I feel your pain. To get out of doing some chores one Saturday, I told my mom I had a big homework project to do with my friend Mark. Then I went to Mark's house to play baseball. My mom called Mark's mom to check on how the project was coming along. I had to lie to Mark's mom, too. Then we had to go sit in Mark's room and pretend we were working on homework that we didn't even have!

Here's what I learned. When you tell one lie, you often have to tell another lie to make that first lie make sense. Pretty soon, you are telling a whole lot of lies. The more lies you tell, the less sense they start to make. Telling lies doesn't really work very well.

Sorry, fella, but I think you have to tell your mom that you made Bob up. Tell her you're sorry for breaking the glass. Go ahead, and tell the truth from now on—it's much easier to remember!

Frank

Dear Frank,

My mom and dad are divorced, and my dad has a new girlfriend. I think they are going to get married. My mom asked me if I like my dad's new girlfriend. I do like her, but I don't want to hurt my mom's feelings. What do I say?

Keesha

Dear Keesha,

Boy, this is a sticky one. I don't have a stepparent myself, but my friend Marcy has both a stepmom and a stepdad. I figure she's an expert, so I asked her about your problem.

Marcy says life with extra parents can be good and bad. When her mom was getting married again, her dad seemed sad and mad. Marcy felt sad and mad, too, but she also felt excited about the wedding. She got to be a junior bridesmaid and wear a cool dress, and her new stepfather was a pretty nice guy. He said he could not be her dad, because she already had a great dad who loved her. Marcy's stepdad asked just to be a part of her life.

The next weekend, Marcy talked to her dad. She told him that she had only one dad–him. She said her new stepdad was nice, but he could never replace her father. Marcy's dad was glad Marcy liked her new stepfather. He wanted her to be happy and to have a home with a stepdad who was a cool guy.

Marcy found a way to be honest about something hard, and it worked out pretty well!

Frank

9

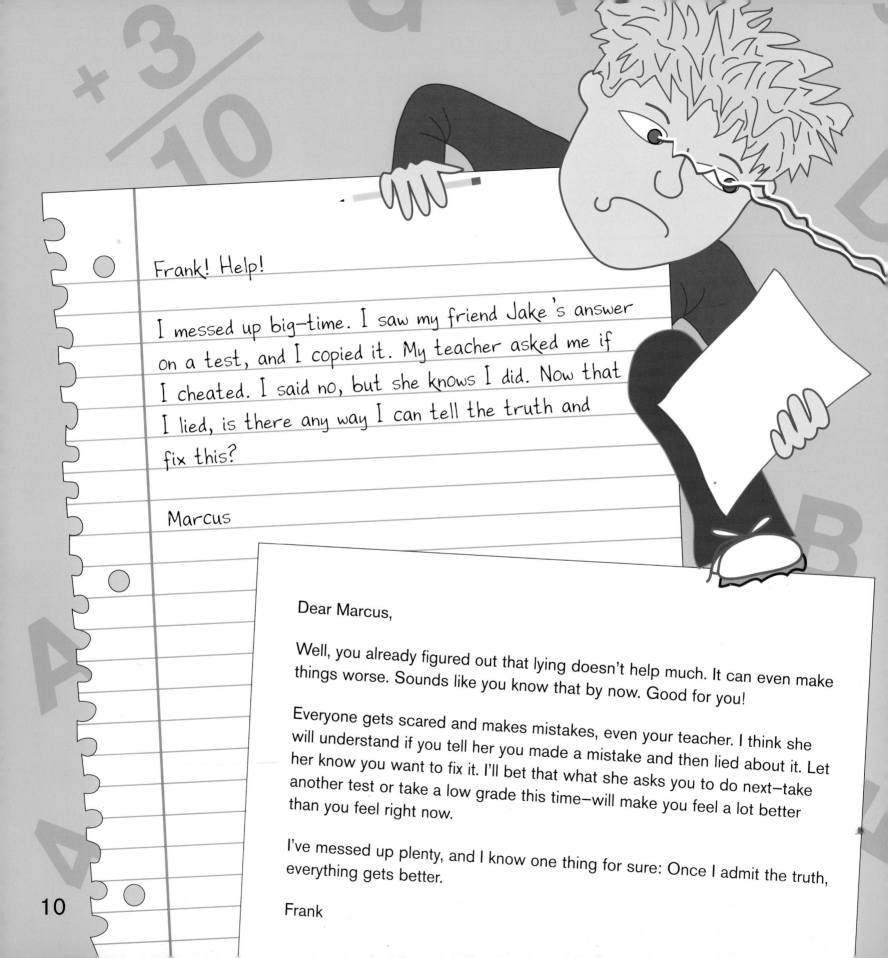

Frank! Help!

I messed up big-time. I saw my friend Jake's answer
on a test, and I copied it. My teacher asked me if
I cheated. I said no, but she knows I did. Now that
I lied, is there any way I can tell the truth and
fix this?

Marcus

Dear Marcus,

Well, you already figured out that lying doesn't help much. It can even make things worse. Sounds like you know that by now. Good for you!

Everyone gets scared and makes mistakes, even your teacher. I think she will understand if you tell her you made a mistake and then lied about it. Let her know you want to fix it. I'll bet that what she asks you to do next—take another test or take a low grade this time—will make you feel a lot better than you feel right now.

I've messed up plenty, and I know one thing for sure: Once I admit the truth, everything gets better.

Frank

Dear Frank,

My grandmother came to our house for dinner, and I told her that my dad says her house smells funny. My dad always says I should tell the truth, and that's what I did. But now my dad is mad at me. I don't get it!

Hannah

Dear Hannah,

Oops! I'll bet your dad's face turned red when you did that. Maybe your grandmother's face did, too!

I went right to my own dad on this one, since I've heard him say that my grandmother's cooking should be against the law. Your story made him smile, Hannah. He said your dad is probably feeling embarrassed, and that's why he acted mad.

My dad says telling the truth is best, but sometimes certain things are better left unsaid. Maybe your grandma's house does smell funny, and both you and your dad know it. Your dad said it to you, and you could say it to him—just don't say it to your grandma. She doesn't need to know her house smells funny. It will just make her feel bad, and there is probably nothing she can do about it, anyway. Sometimes it's better to just zip your lips, and keep quiet.

Frank

Frank,

My friends all like a certain TV show, but I think it's dumb. When we were all talking about it, I said I liked it, too. Why did I do that? Now I feel like I lied.

Darin

Dear Darin,

It seems like the easiest thing to tell the truth about would be yourself, doesn't it? Hey, I know from experience that isn't always how it works.

It seems like my friends and I disagree about a lot of things. We don't like the same foods, the same teachers, or the same TV shows. Sure, sometimes my friend Stan, who loves to play the guitar, teases me about reading books about dinosaurs. He thinks they're boring. I think they're great, so I just laugh and keep reading them. Stan is still my friend. In fact, I think he likes having a friend who reads dinosaur books. I know I like having a friend who knows so much about guitars.

So, Darin, try telling your friends the truth about what you like and don't like. My guess is they'll still be your friends. Maybe some kid you don't know yet will hear you and say, "That show is dumb!" and you'll make a new friend!

Frank

Frank,

My friend Anna plays on our soccer team, and she's awful! She's a great friend but a crummy goalkeeper. Sometimes she asks me, "Am I bad at this, or is the other team really good?" What am I supposed to say? I don't want to hurt her feelings.

16

Sophie

Dear Sophie,

Great question, Sophie. Boy, we all have this problem now and then. Friends want the truth from friends, but what do you do when the truth hurts?

The truth might be painful to your friend, but how you say it doesn't have to be. OK, so Anna is a rotten goalkeeper. That's the harsh truth, but you don't have to speak to her harshly about it.

Let's say she let in the winning goal. You wouldn't say, "Gee, Anna, any idiot could have stopped that one!" Instead, you'd say, "You seem to have trouble stopping those high, corner shots. Maybe you and I can practice those together sometime."

You wouldn't say, "Anna! Why do you even bother to play soccer when you stink at it?" Instead, you'd say, "OK, so maybe soccer isn't your best sport, but you sure are a great ice-skater."

My dad says being honest without hurting someone's feelings is called being tactful. Tact is something good for friends to know how to use.

Good luck!

Frank

17

Dear Frank,

My friend T.J. tells the truth all the time. He thinks he's a stand-up comedian or something. He thinks he's being so funny when he tells people they are fat, ugly, stinky, or wear dumb clothes. Is T.J. too honest?

Chris

Dear Chris,

There is honesty like, "I'm the one who broke the dish." Then there is honesty like T.J.'s, which is pretty rude.

Sure, we're all told to tell the truth about things that happen. However, what we think about how someone dresses or looks is really just our opinion—our own, private idea of what looks cool and what doesn't. With opinions, there is no right or wrong, no real truth or lie. We each get to have our own ideas.

What T.J. is doing is sharing all of his opinions with everybody. If a kid asks T.J., "Do you like my new glasses?" then maybe T.J. has to say something. If the kid with glasses doesn't ask, it's just mean of T.J. to shout, "What dumb glasses!"

Keeping your opinion to yourself about something like your friend's new glasses is not being dishonest. It's just letting your friend make his own decisions. Somebody should tell that to T.J.

Frank

Dear Frank,

I was playing at my friend Sammy's house. He started lighting matches in his living room. I got scared and went home. I told my mom, and she called Sammy's mom. Sammy got in trouble. Now he won't talk to me. Telling the truth makes bad things happen! Should I ever tell the truth again?

Brian

Dear Brian,

I'm glad you wrote to me.

What Sammy was doing should have scared you. It wasn't safe, and you knew it. Your mother called his mother because Sammy could have burned their house down. That's really serious! Your mom was trying to help. Sammy's mother got mad at Sammy because Sammy did something dangerous. She didn't want him to get hurt. Sounds to me like everyone did the right thing—except Sammy.

Sammy can't stay mad forever. Ask him over to play his favorite video game. If he tries to play with matches again, you already know what to do.

Frank

Dear Frank,

My uncle Pete has cancer. He is in a wheelchair and has lost his hair. My dad asks if I want to visit him. I don't know if I do. I love my uncle, but I don't like how he looks now. Plus, dad gets sad when we are there. I would rather stay home and play a video game. I don't know what to tell my dad.

Tyler

Dear Tyler,

It must be hard for you to see your uncle when he feels so bad. It must be hard for you to see your dad get so sad, too. Of course it would be easier to just stay home and play a video game.

It can be hard to figure out the right answer. Being honest doesn't mean you have an answer. It just means you should say what you feel. If you are feeling confused, maybe that's the best thing to say right now.

Try telling your dad what you wrote me. Tell him it's hard to see him sad, and it's hard to see your uncle when he's so sick. Tell him you're confused. That's being honest. I'll bet your dad can help you figure out what to do.

Frank

Dear Frank,

I'll tell you, but I don't want to tell anyone else. I am afraid of bees. I tell my friends I am allergic to bees, and that I have to go to the hospital if one stings me. That isn't true. I'm just afraid of bees. Am I doing something wrong?

Carla

24

Dear Carla,

Beekeepers love bees, and we all love honey, but bees make most of us nervous. Who wants to get stung? Not me! Don't feel silly for being scared.

Everyone has something that scares them—bugs, snakes, thunderstorms, something. Me? I don't like bats. I know they eat mosquitoes, but I still don't like them. One got in my bedroom once, and I have to admit, I yelled.

Here's the problem with saying you are allergic. If a bee ever does sting you, everyone will think you need to be rushed to the hospital. You don't want to make everyone else scared. Plus, you don't want to go to the hospital if you don't need to go.

You don't like bees. Maybe you think no one will pay attention to how you feel unless you make it into something bigger—like an allergy. Carla, if you say you don't like bees, that's enough for me! I'm sure it's enough for your friends, too.

Frank

25

Dear Frank,

My friend Amy is so bossy that I don't want to play with her anymore. When she asks me to come over, I tell her I am busy. My mom says I need to tell her the truth. Just how do I do that?

Sally

Dear Sally,

I can totally relate! My friend David likes to tease. He calls it goofing around. I call it being mean. He was so mean, I started to like him less. I didn't want to hang out with him. He couldn't read my mind, so he kept calling. My mom said I needed to be honest with David. She said I had to do it without being mean, though.

The next time David called, I was nervous. I wanted to lie and tell him I had to do homework. Instead, I told David I liked him, but his teasing hurt my feelings. I told him I felt bad when we hung out together.

Guess what happened next? David came right over and said he was sorry. He said he was just trying to be funny. He had no idea that what he was doing was hurting my feelings. He also said he would try to stop his teasing.

So go ahead and try to be honest with your friend. I'll bet it will make everything better!

Frank

27

It's Quiz Time ?

Here's a pop quiz that is actually fun. Grab a piece of paper and a pencil. Relax! You can't get a bad grade on this one.

1. Telling the truth:
   - A. is always fun and easy.
   - B. can be hard to do.
   - C. gives you a rash.

2. Cheating on a test:
   - A. is great if you don't get caught.
   - B. is great even if you do get caught.
   - C. can make you feel bad about what you did.

3. If you mess up:
   - A. say you're sorry, and try to fix it.
   - B. hide under the bed for a year.
   - C. tell yourself that you are really dumb.

4. When your friends like a TV show you don't like:
   - A. watch it, and pretend to laugh.
   - B. unplug the television.
   - C. say it's not your favorite, and do something else.

5. When a friend is rude:
   - A. slam the door in his face.
   - B. stick out your tongue at his dog.
   - C. tell him he's hurting your feelings.

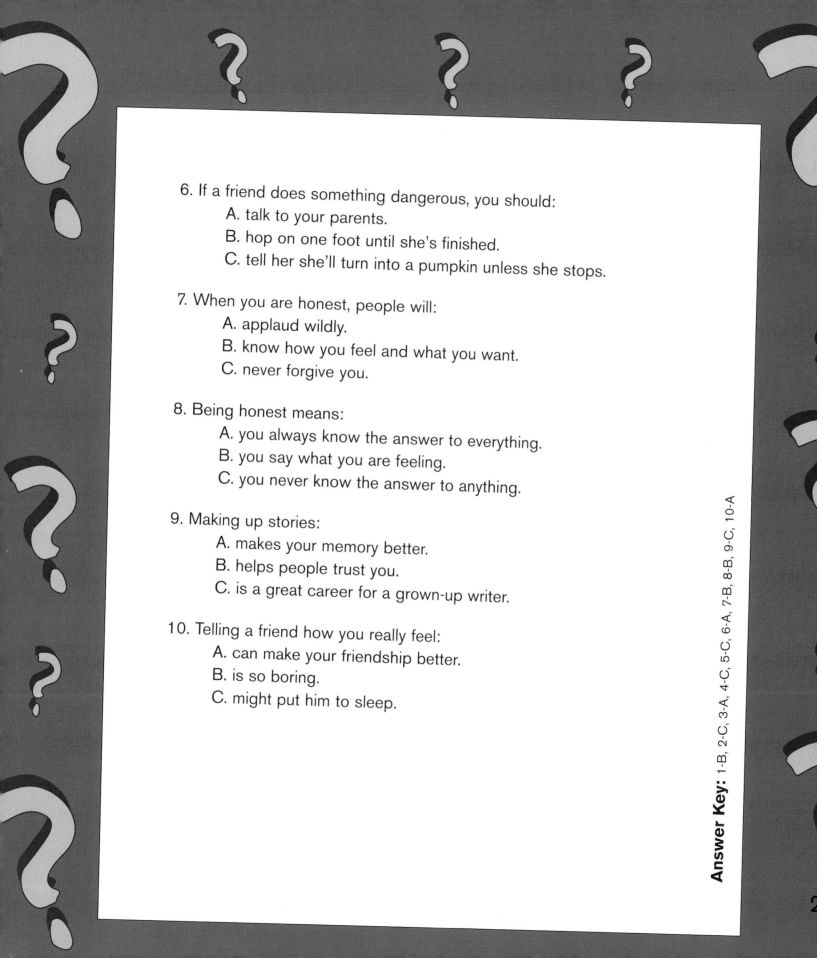

6. If a friend does something dangerous, you should:
   A. talk to your parents.
   B. hop on one foot until she's finished.
   C. tell her she'll turn into a pumpkin unless she stops.

7. When you are honest, people will:
   A. applaud wildly.
   B. know how you feel and what you want.
   C. never forgive you.

8. Being honest means:
   A. you always know the answer to everything.
   B. you say what you are feeling.
   C. you never know the answer to anything.

9. Making up stories:
   A. makes your memory better.
   B. helps people trust you.
   C. is a great career for a grown-up writer.

10. Telling a friend how you really feel:
    A. can make your friendship better.
    B. is so boring.
    C. might put him to sleep.

Answer Key: 1-B, 2-C, 3-A, 4-C, 5-C, 6-A, 7-B, 8-B, 9-C, 10-A

One person's honesty can change the entire world, and Rachel Carson did just that. She told the truth about how people were damaging the environment. Nobody worried about pollution or litter. Nobody worried about recycling, either. Rachel changed people's thinking.

Rachel grew up on a farm in Pennsylvania. Her mother taught her to love the plants and animals around her. She went to college and studied to become a marine biologist. She was a good writer and wrote two books about the ocean. Rachel also studied what was happening to life on land. She learned that the sprays and chemicals used to kill pesky bugs were also hurting and killing birds and other animals.

Rachel Carson wrote a book in 1962 called *Silent Spring.* Everyone was talking about Rachel's book. The word was out: Using certain chemicals to kill bugs can hurt lots of other living things. Rachel had people thinking about pollution and harmful chemicals. People started to take action and help the environment.

The companies that made bug-killing chemicals were mad. Farmers who needed to keep bugs off their crops were mad, too. However, Rachel was brave and honest. She knew the same chemicals that hurt bugs could hurt people. She said we have to be careful about what we spray in the air and pour into the water.

Companies had to change the way they made chemicals. Farmers found new ways to kill bugs. Laws were made about keeping the air and water clean. People learned how to reuse, or recycle, garbage and not waste so much stuff. Thanks to Rachel Carson's honesty, people have tried to protect the environment instead of hurting it.

Words to Know

Here are some of my favorite words and expressions from today's letters.

advice–suggestions from people who think they know what you should do about a problem

allergic–some things, like bee stings or pollen in the air, can make people feel sick; many allergies make you sneeze

cancer–a serious illness; people with cancer see the doctor a lot and go to the hospital for care; some cancer medicines make people lose their hair

career–a job; when you get older, you have to go to work every day instead of going to school

confused–feeling and thinking lots of different things at once; sometimes you need to stop and think quietly for a while to help the confused feeling go away

stepdad–the man who marries your mother if something happens to your dad

stepmom–the woman who marries your dad if something happens to your mom

tact–a way of being honest without hurting someone's feelings

To Learn More

At the Library

Blair, Eric. *The Boy Who Cried Wolf*. Minneapolis: Picture Window Books, 2004.

Cosby, Bill. *My Big Lie*. New York: Scholastic, 1999.

McKissack, Patricia C. *The Honest-to-Goodness Truth*. New York: Atheneum, 2000.

On the Web

FactHound offers a safe, fun way to find Web sites related to this book. All of the sites on FactHound have been researched by our staff. *www.facthound.com*

1. Visit the FactHound home page
2. Enter a search word related to this book, or type in this special code: 1404806199.
3. Click on the FETCH IT button.

Your trusty FactHound will fetch the best Web sites for you!

Index

Books in This Series

- **Do I Have To? Kids Talk About Responsibility**

- **How Could You? Kids Talk About Trust**

- **I Can Do It! Kids Talk About Courage**

- **Is That True? Kids Talk About Honesty**

- **May I Help You? Kids Talk About Caring**

- **No Fair! Kids Talk About Fairness**

- **Pitch In! Kids Talk About Cooperation**

- **Let's Get Along! Kids Talk About Tolerance**

- **Treat Me Right! Kids Talk About Respect**

- **Want to Play? Kids Talk About Friendliness**

- **We Live Here Too! Kids Talk About Good Citizenship**

- **You First! Kids Talk About Consideration**